"Against All Odds, Full Circle"

By

Michael L Dennis

***This work was inspired by the music and lyrics of such artists as Guns N' Roses, Phil Collins, Journey, Jeff Buckley, Foreigner, Ray LaMontagne, REO Speedwagon, Leona Lewis, Whitesnake, Heart, The Airborne Toxic Event, specifically their songs: "Is This Love," "Open Arms," "Highway to the Sun," I Want to know what love is" "Waiting for a Girl Like You," Sometime Around Midnight", Against All Odds", All I Wanna Do". While elements of this book were influenced by the themes and emotions expressed in the original works, the content has been rephrased and adapted to align with copyright requirements and original expression. Any resemblance to the original lyrics or themes is intended as homage and does not replicate the original work.*

About the Author

Michael L. Dennis, originally from Lake Hiawatha, New Jersey, now resides in Canton, Georgia, where he continues to find inspiration in both the memories of the past and the experiences of life's current journey. His writing spans a wide range of genres, reflecting his diverse interests and imagination.

From the chilling depths of horror and the supernatural in The Clearing *Eliza*, to the tender exploration of love and heartbreak in Against All Odds: Full Circle, Michael's stories capture the complexities of the human experience. His science fiction novel Expect Delays challenges the boundaries of reality, while his children's book The King's Chair celebrates the boundless power of a

When Michael isn't crafting new stories, he can be found at home, drawing inspiration from the world around him and embracing the creative process.

Prologue

The first time Dennis saw Katarina, it was like the world had shifted on its axis. He was a man living in a predictable routine, comfortable in his safe and familiar patterns.

She was a whirlwind of vibrant energy and passion, a force of nature that swept him off his feet and made him question everything he thought he knew about himself. He was a man who had never truly believed in love until she came along.

But love, as they all know, can be a fickle thing, a delicate dance between two souls. The future stretched out before them, promising limitless possibilities, but the path to their happily ever after was not as clear as they'd hoped. Life, with its unpredictable twists and turns, had other plans.

Just a Friend

The hum of the office was a constant, a low drone that Dennis had come to tune out. He'd been at the marketing firm for almost three years and had settled into a routine, a predictability that had become as comforting as it was dull. He was good at his job, but he wasn't passionate about it. He was, however, passionate about Katarina, a woman he'd met at a work social gathering a few months back. The fire of their connection had simmered down a bit – hesitant to "dip their pen in company ink". They'd both agreed to keep it casual, a flirtation that never went further. They'd both told their friends, "friendly/professional," and while they'd both known it was more than that, they'd kept the boundaries clear.

One Friday afternoon, Dennis was hunched over his computer, trying to decipher the latest marketing data. The numbers danced before his eyes, but his mind was adrift, lost in thoughts of Katarina. She had this way of lighting up a room, her presence a spark that drew him in. He couldn't help but steal glances at her desk across the office, watching the way she tilted her head when she was absorbed in work, the way her hair fell over her shoulders, the way her eyes crinkled when she laughed.

He looked up as the office door opened, and there she was, Katarina, walking in with a stack of files. She saw him staring, and for a moment, their eyes met, a silent exchange of amusement passing between them.

He offered a small smile, which she returned with a playful wink. "Busy day?" she asked, leaning on his desk, her voice barely above a whisper.

"Just trying to make sense of this mess," Dennis replied, gesturing towards the jumbled spreadsheet. "You know how it is, marketing data - it's like trying to decipher hieroglyphics."

Katarina laughed, her hand coming up to rest on his arm, a touch that sent a jolt of electricity through him. "Sounds like a real thrill," she said, her voice husky with laughter. "Maybe I should try my hand at some of that magic."

He stood, surprised by the sudden shift in the air, the electricity that had always crackled between them feeling more intense now. "Maybe I need a little bit of your magic to help me out," he said, his voice a little hoarse. "Maybe we could grab a coffee after work, and you could give me a crash course."

They both knew it was a bit forward, a flirtation that dared to edge out of the boundaries they'd set. The question lingered in the air – were they ready to "dip their pen"?

Katarina's eyes widened, a slight flush rising on her cheeks. "I don't know," she said, her voice a little softer now, a hint of shyness in her tone. "What about this 'keeping it professional' thing we've got going?"

He chuckled, the heat of the moment making him feel bolder. "professional? Well, maybe "professional" needs a little bit of a downgrade."

She laughed, her hand lingering on his arm, their eyes locked in a moment before she leaned back, a hint of mischief in her smile. "Maybe you're right," she said, the words almost a whisper. "But maybe just a little."

That night, they shared a quiet dinner, the conversation flowing as easily as the wine. The boundaries they'd kept before seemed to fade, replaced by a shared sense of connection. It was almost as if they had always been on the precipice, a single step away from acknowledging the undeniable truth that their friendship was more. Something in the past held them back, a fear of what might happen, a fear of disrupting the comfortable routine they'd built for themselves, but now, that was gone, replaced with the romance and desires only read about in books.

But that all changed a few years later after Dennis and Katarina broke up. The news hit Emily hard, a wave of sadness washing over her as she watched her friend, a good friend, struggle so mightily, a fragile shell of the man she'd known. She felt a surge of protectiveness, a need to be there for him. She knew she couldn't replace Katarina in his heart, but she could be there for him, offering him comfort and support.

The first time she saw Dennis after their breakup, he looked lost, a shadow of the man who had once radiated such energy and confidence. She felt a deep pang of sympathy, a desire to be more than just a friend. She had been "just a friend", a role she had comfortably played, but at that moment, she realized that she needed to be more. She needed to be both a vocal support, a shoulder to cry on, and a physical support, a source of comfort.

"You, okay?" She asked, taking his hand in hers, the warmth of her touch a small ray of hope in the darkness he carried. "It's okay to not be okay."

He looked up at her, his eyes red-rimmed, the sadness he carried heavy on his face. He'd never truly seen her vulnerability, the gentle strength beneath her playful exterior. He saw it now, and it resonated deeply with him.

"I'm not okay," he admitted, his voice raw, the honesty a relief during the turmoil he carried. "I don't know what to do."

She smiled, a soft, reassuring smile, a promise of comfort and understanding. "I'm here, Dennis. I'm always here. You're not alone."

That night, as he held her, the warmth of her presence a bandage on his wounded soul, Dennis knew that he'd found more than a friend in Emily. He'd found a haven, a safe space, a source of comfort and strength, and he knew that he could lean on her. He was no longer alone.

"Patience"

Dennis sat on the cold stone steps outside his apartment in Lake Caldwell, NJ, the twilight settling over the city like a blanket of sorrow. The dim light of the fading sun cast long shadows across the street, but Dennis was lost in the darkness of his own mind, his thoughts circling back to the only place they ever seemed to go—Katarina.

It had been weeks since she'd left, weeks since he'd watched her walk out the door without a fight. And yet, she hadn't left him. She was everywhere. In the quiet hum of the refrigerator, in the muffled footsteps of strangers passing by. She was the echo that refused to fade, the presence that haunted his every waking moment.

He swallowed the lump in his throat, forcing himself to remember the last time he saw her—Katarina, moving through the street like a vision. Her smile had been fleeting, but it cut him deeply as if the world had given him a glimpse of what he'd lost just to remind him of the pain.

The day she walked out still felt like yesterday. She had said she needed space and that they were moving too fast, too recklessly. "Just give it time," she'd told him. "We both need to breathe." But Dennis had never been good at waiting. He'd spent his whole life charging forward, determined to take what he wanted. But now, he felt powerless, stranded in a life that had grown empty without her.

"Said woman, take it slow, and things will be just fine…" The words echoed in his head, a line from that old song she loved, the one they used to play in the car when the world felt right and the future seemed limitless. But now the lyrics felt like a cruel joke. Patience had never been his virtue, and Katarina had been his only exception.

His hands trembled as he pulled out his phone, scrolling through their old texts, the messages now a painful reminder of what once was. Her words still brought him comfort and agony all at once, and as his thumb hovered over her name, he felt the weight of his helplessness crash down on him. How many nights had he sat there, waiting for her to reach out? How many times had he told himself that this would pass, that she would come back, that love like theirs didn't just vanish into thin air?

But love wasn't enough, was it?

Dennis sighed, the breath heavy with the burden of weeks spent pretending he was fine, of telling himself that he could wait for her—no matter how long it took. But it wasn't the waiting that killed him. It was the fear that maybe, just maybe, she wouldn't come back at all.

"I sit here on the stairs 'cause I'd rather be alone," the song played again in his mind. Alone. That word echoed through the empty spaces of his life where Katarina once fit so perfectly. He didn't want anyone else. He couldn't imagine filling the void she had left with another person, another set of hands to hold, another pair of eyes to look into. No, he would rather wait forever for her than settle for someone else's half-hearted love.

But as the weeks dragged on, patience felt like a slow form of torture. Every morning he woke up without her felt heavier than the last. Every night without her voice felt colder. He had started to doubt whether waiting was a sign of strength or a form of surrender. Was he holding onto hope, or was he slowly letting go of it?

He leaned forward, burying his face in his hands, his heart aching with a pain he couldn't name. He wanted to call her, but what if she was with another, another who was getting the best of her both mentally and physically? I wanted to call, to beg her to come back, to tell her that the space between them was killing him. But he could hear her voice, even now, whispering in his ear, "Take it slow, Dennis. We need this time. Trust me." And he did trust her. He trusted her more than he had ever trusted anyone. But how long could he keep trusting that time would heal them, that distance would bring them back together instead of tearing them apart?

"All we need is just a little patience," she had said. But patience wasn't easy, especially on nights like this, when the silence screamed louder than any words ever could. He couldn't stop thinking about her, couldn't stop wanting her. The need to hold her, to hear her laugh, to kiss her one more time—it was suffocating.

A tear slipped down his cheek, and he didn't bother wiping it away. He let it fall, let it mix with the bitter cold of the evening air. Maybe this was how it had to be. Maybe he needed to break down completely before he could rise again. But as much as he tried to tell himself that he was strong enough to endure this, a part of him knew that he was slowly unraveling.

The city lights flickered on one by one, casting a dull glow over the streets below. He stared at them, wishing he could find comfort in their warmth, but all he saw was a world that had kept moving without him. Everything was still, and yet nothing felt right.

"You and I got what it takes to make it," her voice played again in his mind like a distant lullaby he no longer believed in. They had shared something real, something deep, something that he couldn't shake no matter how hard he tried. But now, all he had were memories. Memories that lingered like ghosts, haunting every corner of his apartment, every inch of his soul.

He wiped his eyes and stood, his legs heavy beneath him. He wasn't sure how much longer he could do this—how much longer he could wait for someone who might never come back. But what other choice did he have? He had already given her everything. What was a little more time?

As he turned and walked back inside, the door closing softly behind him, Dennis whispered into the darkness, "I'll wait for you, Katarina. I'll wait as long as it takes. Because all we need... is just a little patience."

But deep down, he wondered if patience was enough to save him from the emptiness that grew with every passing day.

Against All Odds

The early morning light filtered through the thin curtains of Dennis's bedroom, casting a soft glow on the walls. He lay awake, staring at the ceiling, his mind heavy with the weight of another sleepless night. The emptiness that had settled into his life since Katarina left felt like a constant companion, following him through every moment, every breath.

How can I just let you leave, disappearing without a trace

The words in his mind echoed, a haunting that he couldn't escape. He had watched Katarina pack her things and had stood there as she walked out the door without a single word of protest. Now, in the quiet of his apartment, he regretted his silence. He regretted letting her go without a fight.

While I stand here talking every breath without you

He sat up in bed, his hair as lost as he was, and looked around the room. The space felt so empty now, devoid of the life and warmth Katarina had brought with her. Every corner held a memory, and every memory was a reminder of what he'd lost. She had been the one person who truly understood him, who knew him in ways no one else ever had.

He reached for his phone, needing to hear a familiar voice, a voice that wouldn't remind him of what he'd lost. He dialed Emily's number, his thumb hovering over the call button. He hadn't spoken to Emily in weeks, not since before Katarina left. Emily was a friend from work, someone he'd always felt comfortable around, someone who always seemed to understand him. He wasn't sure why he was calling her now, but he needed to hear her voice, to hear about her life, a life that didn't include him anymore.

As Emily's voice crackled through the speaker, he realized he'd been avoiding her, not out of malice but out of fear. He was afraid that he might start to feel something real with Emily, something he wasn't sure he was ready for. He was afraid that he might lose her, just like he'd lost Katarina. And he wasn't sure he could handle that, not right now, not when he was still so raw, so lost in the wreckage of his heart.

As he finally dragged himself out of bed after a brief but good talk with Emily, his eyes caught sight of a note Katarina had left behind, stuck to the fridge door. It was something she had written long before they had parted ways, a simple reminder to buy groceries, but it was her handwriting, her words. The sight of it made his chest tighten, a painful reminder of her absence.

How can you just walk away from this, While all I can do is watch you go?

He had tried to convince himself that her leaving had been for the best, that they both needed time apart to figure things out. But now, standing in the emptiness of his apartment, it felt like a lie. He had been holding onto the hope that she would come back, that they could somehow fix what had been broken between them. But each day that passed only deepened the void she had left behind.

So look at me now—there's nothing here, just empty space

Dennis stepped out onto his small balcony, letting the cool morning air wash over him. He closed his eyes, leaning against the railing, and allowed himself to fully feel the weight of his grief. He had lost more than just Katarina—he had lost the version of himself that he had been with her. Without her, he felt like a shell of the person he once was, fragile and worn down by the relentless tide of days that blurred together.

And all that remains is the memory of your face

He had replayed their last moments together in his mind so many times, wishing he could turn back the clock, make her stay, make her see how much she meant to him. But now, all he had were memories— and the painful realization that waiting for her to come back was like waiting for something that would never happen.

The thought of you returning feels impossible, but it's a truth I have face.

Dennis knew that the chances of her returning were slim. He had watched her leave without looking back, and though every part of him had wanted to run after her, he hadn't. Now, as the weeks turned into months, the reality of her absence was settling in. The odds were against him, and yet, he couldn't let go of the hope that maybe, somehow, she would find her way back to him.

I wish I could make you turn around, see my tears

There was so much he hadn't said to her, so much he had kept bottled up inside. He had always been the one to hold back, to keep his emotions in check, but now, as he stood on the balcony staring out at the world below, he wished he had let her see just how much he needed her. He wished he had fought for her.

There's so much I still need to say, so many reasons why

Dennis took a deep breath, trying to steady himself. The pain was still there, raw and unrelenting, but he knew he couldn't keep living like this. He had to find a way to move forward, even if it meant accepting that Katarina wasn't coming back.

But you were the only one who ever really knew me

As he stepped back inside, the apartment felt just as empty as it had been before. The note on the fridge caught his eye again, a small reminder of the life they had once shared. He stared at it for a long moment, the pain still fresh, but there was a flicker of something else— a quiet determination to keep going, to keep living, even without her.

He walked towards the note, fully intending to rip it into a thousand little pieces, "but what if this is the last physical memory I'll ever have of you?" Dennis calmed his emotions and neatly placed it out of sight.

He knew the odds were against him, but that didn't mean he had to stop hoping. Maybe, just maybe, there was still a chance that she would come back. And until then, he would keep going, keep holding onto the memory of her, because it was all he had left.

Take a hard look at me now, because here I'll remain

Dennis knew he had a long way to go and that the road ahead would be difficult. But he also knew that he wasn't ready to give up, not yet.

He would wait, against all odds, because that was the only chance he had left.

"Forget Her"

Dennis wandered the streets late at night, the familiar chill of autumn settling into his bones. The streets of Lake Caldwell were nearly empty, the occasional car passing by, but nothing interrupted the silence that hung heavy around him. It had been months since Katarina left, yet her presence clung to every shadow, every corner of his mind. Forgetting her was a battle he lost daily.

He found himself at the park—their park—the place where they'd spent countless hours together, laughing, talking, kissing under the trees by the lake. The memories felt like acid now, burning his heart from the inside. He sat down on the cold bench, staring out at the water, his breath visible in the cool night air. Every ripple on the lake's surface reminded him of the way she had smiled, the way her laugh would light up his world.

But now, there was only emptiness. She had moved on. She had found a way to leave the memories behind, to let go of him, but Dennis… Dennis still carried her with him, like a weight that grew heavier with each passing day. She had become the ghost that haunted his waking life, a constant reminder of what he'd lost.

"Don't fool yourself," he whispered to the night, his voice barely audible. "She was heartache from the moment that you met her." The words felt bitter, but they were the truth. Katarina had always been a storm—beautiful, fierce, and devastating. She had swept into his life and turned everything upside down, leaving him to pick up the pieces when she left.

And then there was Emily.

Dennis pulled his phone from his pocket, staring at the screen where her name sat, waiting for him to make a move. Emily wasn't like Katarina. She was steady and grounded, and she didn't ask for more than he could give. She had stepped into his life just when the ache of losing Katarina felt unbearable, offering him comfort and the physical closeness he craved. But she wasn't the cure. She was never going to be the cure.

He hesitated before typing a message.

"You up?"

The reply was instant, almost like she was expecting the call. "Yeah. Can I come over?"

Dennis pocketed his phone, stood up from the bench and made his way back to his apartment. The truth was, he didn't want to be alone tonight. He didn't want to sit in the silence of his apartment, staring at the walls that held so many memories of Katarina. He needed someone—anyone—to fill the space she had left behind, even if it was just for a little while.

By the time he got home, Emily was already waiting for him at the door. She smiled softly as he let her in, the kind of smile that didn't demand anything, that simply offered presence and warmth. Dennis appreciated that about her. She didn't push. She didn't try to fix him. She just was.

"Hey, you're okay, ok?" she said quietly as she slipped off her jacket, while hanging it on the back of a chair. She already knew the answer, but it was her way of acknowledging the unspoken truth while inserting a bit of confidence.

Dennis gave a slight nod, not trusting himself to speak. He wasn't okay. He hadn't been okay since the day Katarina had walked out of his life. But Emily knew that, and she never asked for more than he could give.

They moved through the small, familiar motions. She wrapped her arms around him, pulling him into a quiet embrace, and for a moment, Dennis let himself sink into her touch. Her warmth was a comfort he didn't deserve, but he needed it all the same.

He pressed his face into her hair, inhaling the scent of her shampoo, almost losing himself in that moment and almost losing his self-control.

But it wasn't enough.

No matter how close Emily held him, no matter how much she gave, it wasn't Katarina. His mind was always half somewhere else, replaying old moments with a woman who had already left him behind. He hated himself for it—hated the way he used Emily to fill the void, knowing it was temporary, knowing it wasn't fair to either of them.

They ended up on the couch; Emily curled up against him, her hand resting on his chest. It was a comfortable intimacy, one that soothed the physical loneliness for both but did nothing for the deeper ache inside him. Dennis absentmindedly stroked her hair, staring at the ceiling, his thoughts far away.

"It's okay if you're thinking about her, you know." Emily's voice broke through the silence, soft but steady. She wasn't angry; she never was, but her words held a sadness that Dennis had come to recognize.

He didn't answer, and he didn't need to; the silence was confirmation enough.

Emily sat up slightly, her eyes searching his face. "You don't have to explain, you know. I get it."

Dennis swallowed; guilt for that very moment was absent and no longer gnawing at him. "You do?" he muttered. It was the only thing he could say at that moment.

Emily gave a small, sad smile, slightly tilting her head and leaned back against him. "I understand what all of this is right now; I understand."

She knew. She had always known that she was a placeholder, that Dennis's heart was somewhere else. And she had accepted that role, the role of someone who could be there when he needed, without the expectation of more. But that didn't make it any easier.

"I just don't know how to stop thinking about her," Dennis admitted, his voice barely above a whisper. "No matter what I do, she's always… there."

Emily didn't say anything for a moment, letting his words settle in the quiet room. Then, she reached up and gently took his hand. "You're not ready to let her go. That's okay."

"But it's not fair to you," Dennis said, his throat tight.

"I'm not asking for fair," Emily replied. "I'm just asking to be here. For now."

Dennis felt a knot form in his chest. He didn't deserve Emily's understanding. He didn't deserve her quiet, patient presence. But here she was, offering him comfort without asking for anything in return, "was it selfish to take it?" he thought to himself.

They sat in silence for a long time, the only sound in the room the faint ticking of the clock on the wall.

The night stretched on, and eventually, they made their way to bed together, the physical closeness offering some relief, though Dennis knew it would never be enough, was coming at the right time. All his emotional love making that was always reserved for Katarina was placed upon Emily.

During those intimate moments, as his passion took over and ran deep, Emily, for a moment, wondered if he was making love to her or Katarina. She came to her senses; she knew.

They kept at it for what seemed and eternity, both taking control at times.

It was, for both, an opportunity to fulfill inner fantasies and dive into a world we all have deep inside our minds.

As they lay there, Emily resting against him, her breathing finally slowing and steady; Dennis stared into the darkness. His hand rested on her back, tracing absent patterns against her skin. He appreciated her warmth, the softness of her body against his, but his mind was still a thousand miles away, lost in memories of Katarina.

He closed his eyes, trying to let the physical connection between him and Emily distract him from the storm in his heart. But the storm raged on, and Katarina's face lingered behind his eyelids, as vivid and painful as ever.

He had tried so hard to forget her, but she was a part of him now, woven into his very being. No matter how much time passed, no matter how many nights he spent with Emily, he couldn't escape the truth—Katarina was still the one he longed for.

Dennis sighed deeply, his breath stirring the quiet of the room. Emily shifted slightly beside him but didn't wake. He pressed a kiss to her forehead, a gesture of gratitude for something he didn't deserve, and settled back into the pillows.

But even as the night wore on, and even as Emily's presence provided a temporary balm for the loneliness, Dennis knew the truth. He wasn't healing. He wasn't moving on. He was stuck, trapped between the woman who had left him and the one who stayed, knowing that no amount of physical comfort could heal the wounds that Katarina had left behind.

Tomorrow, he'd wake up next to Emily, and for a few hours, the pain would be dulled. But the ache of missing Katarina, of wanting her back, would return, as it always did.

And no matter how hard he tried, Dennis couldn't forget her.

Katarina's Homecoming

The familiar scent of honeysuckle filled the air as Katarina walked down her childhood street. The brick houses, each with their own porch swing and manicured lawns felt like a warm embrace. She'd been gone for three years, chasing a dream of self-discovery in the bustling streets of California, but Lake Caldwell always held a special place in her heart. It was the place where she'd spent the first eighteen years of her life, a place where she'd learned to ride her bike, built sandcastles on the shore of the lake, and fallen in love with the quiet beauty of small-town life.

The move to California had been exhilarating, a whirlwind of new experiences, a chance to shed her small-town skin and embrace a world of endless possibilities. She'd found herself immersed in the vibrant energy of the city, trying her hand at everything from the debilitating experience of the casting couch, the bore of being a bank teller, to joining a rock band as an assistant. She'd met people from all walks of life, each one different from the next, each one offering a unique perspective on the world.

But beneath the surface of those thrilling experiences, a quiet ache lingered. She missed the familiarity of her childhood home, the comforting routine of life in Lake Caldwell, and the sense of belonging she'd felt growing up. She missed her parents, her friends, and the simple joys of life that she'd taken for granted before she'd left.

The city, for all its glamour and excitement, felt like a stage, a place where everyone was playing a role. She'd felt like a character in a movie, constantly trying to figure out who she was supposed to be. But in Lake Caldwell, she was simply Katarina.

The turning point came on her 19th birthday. She was sitting on her porch swing, staring out at the lake, the setting sun casting a golden glow across the water. She'd been on a date the night before, an aspiring actor she'd met at an audition, but she hadn't felt a spark, a connection. Instead, she'd felt a growing sense of disillusionment. The city that had once seemed like a haven of dreams felt like a trap, a place where she was constantly trying to impress, to be someone she wasn't.

That night, under the soft light of the moon, she'd decided. She was going home.

It wasn't an easy decision. Part of her wanted to stay, to keep chasing her dreams, to see where the city would take her. But another part of her, the part that yearned for familiarity and comfort, knew that she was where she belonged. She needed to be closer to her roots, to reconnect with the people who loved her, to find her place in the world.

She returned to Lake Caldwell with a newfound clarity and a sense of purpose. She enrolled at the local college, where she majored in marketing, a subject that sparked a passion in her. She found a job at a small marketing firm and quickly excelled. She made new friends, reconnected with old ones, and felt a sense of belonging she hadn't felt in years.

But she hadn't forgotten California. It had been a valuable experience, a journey of self-discovery that had ultimately led her back to where she truly belonged. She'd learned who she was, what she wanted, and that sometimes, the best way to find yourself is to go back to your roots.

One day, as she sat at her desk, reviewing a new marketing campaign, Dennis walked in, a new hire at the firm. She was instantly intrigued by his quiet confidence and his dark, warm eyes. It was the beginning of something new, and as she watched him settle into his new office space, she had no idea that this handsome stranger would become a source of both joy and heartbreak in her life.

The familiar scent of honeysuckle drifted in through the open window, a reminder of her childhood, her roots, and the journey that had brought her back to where she truly belonged. Lake Caldwell was more than just a town; it was home. And now, she was ready for the next chapter of her story, a story that she knew, with certainty, would be filled with love, laughter, and a sense of belonging she'd never known before.

"Is This Love"

Dennis and Emily spent nearly every waking moment together. What started as a casual spark at work, then a crutch for her friend—had quickly evolved into an intense, almost suffocating closeness. They were inseparable, floating between friends of friends, always invited, always showing up at gatherings together as if bound by some invisible thread. Their love, if it could be called that, was steeped in both joy and heaviness, a dance between what was real and what was convenient.

The days passed in a blur of shared bedsheets and late-night conversations that filled the hollow spaces in Dennis's heart. In the beginning, it was easy. They made love constantly, feverishly, their bodies communicating the needs their words couldn't quite express. Dennis found comfort in Emily's arms, and she in his. Together, they created a kind of rhythm, moving in sync through a haze of weekends away and evenings spent in the company of others. They were always with friends, always at someone's apartment or bar, always surrounded by laughter and clinking glasses. To anyone looking in from the outside, they seemed perfect together.

But beneath the surface, something unspoken simmered. Emily could feel it—a quiet sense of doubt that tugged at her heart in the stillness of the night. She would lie next to Dennis, his arm draped over her like a protective shield and wonder if what they had was more than just a refuge for his broken heart. Her friends began to ask questions, their voices cautious but probing.

"Is this real, Emily?" her closest friend, Sarah, asked one afternoon over coffee. "Or are you just helping him get over her?"

Emily had paused, her fingers tightening around the warm cup in her hands. It was a question she hadn't wanted to face, but it had been gnawing at the back of her mind for weeks. Was this real, or was she still simply a crutch? A temporary fix for a man who was still haunted by the woman who left him.

"I don't know," she admitted quietly, her voice barely audible over the sound of the coffee shop. "I thought it was something. But now..."

Sarah reached out and squeezed her hand gently, the sympathy in her eyes unmissable. "Emily, you deserve to be someone's first choice, not someone's comfort."

That night, the question echoed louder than ever. She and Dennis had been out with friends again, moving from one house party to another, always surrounded by people, laughter, and noise. But even with his arm around her waist, pulling her close, Emily felt the distance between them. She could feel him slipping into his own thoughts, his mind wandering back to a time before her, a life filled with the memory of someone else.

Back at his apartment, they tumbled into bed, their hands moving with an urgency that had become all too familiar. Dennis kissed her like she was the only thing keeping him from drowning, but even as their bodies intertwined, Emily felt a growing emptiness. She wanted him, wanted him more than she had ever wanted anyone. But she couldn't shake the feeling that she was simply filling the cracks left behind by Katarina.

In the early morning light, as Dennis slept soundly beside her, Emily lay awake, staring at the walls. She loved him. She hadn't meant to, but she had fallen for him—deeply, unexpectedly. And now, she wasn't sure if she had been walking into love or if she had simply been stepping into the role of his savior, his safe harbor, while he weathered the storm of his grief.

She remembered the way his face had softened whenever someone mentioned Katarina's name, the way his eyes clouded over with a sadness she couldn't touch. She had tried to ignore it, tried to pretend that it didn't matter, but the truth was inescapable. No matter how many times he held her, no matter how many nights they spent wrapped around each other, she was not Katarina. She would never be Katarina.

One afternoon, she sat alone with her thoughts in a café, her reflection in the window staring back at her. Her mind buzzed with conflicting emotions—love, doubt, happiness, regret. She loved Dennis. She wanted him in her life. But she had come to realize something devastating: she was never going to be his main focal point. She would always be the afterthought, the consolation prize for a heart that was still too broken to love fully.

Her love for him was growing deeper, but so was the pain of knowing that she would never truly have him, not in the way she needed. And the more time they spent together, the clearer it became that this—whatever this was—wasn't enough. Not for either of them.

They were at another gathering that night, this time at a friend's rooftop party. The city skyline stretched out before them, the sun setting in shades of pink and gold. Dennis stood next to her, his hand resting on the small of her back, but Emily felt like she was a million miles away. The laughter of their friends faded into the background as she turned to look at him. He smiled at her, that familiar, easy smile that had once made her heart race. But now, it only filled her with sadness.

"I can't do this anymore, Dennis," she whispered, her voice shaking. The words felt like a knife to her own chest, but they were the truth she could no longer avoid.

Dennis turned to her, confusion and fear flickering in his eyes. "What are you talking about?"

Emily blinked back tears, her throat tightening as she searched for the right words. "I love you. I think I always will. But this… I'm not what you need. And you… you're not fully here with me."

The realization hit him like a punch to the gut. He opened his mouth to protest, to tell her that he was here, that he did love her, but the words wouldn't come. Deep down, he knew she was right.

Emily took a deep breath, trying to steady herself. "I deserve to be someone's first choice, Dennis. And I can't keep pretending that this is enough when it's not."

The weight of her words hung heavy between them, the city lights twinkling behind them like distant stars. Dennis felt his world crumbling around him, the ground slipping out from beneath his feet. He hadn't realized how much he had come to depend on Emily—her presence, her warmth, her love. And now, as she stood before him, ready to walk away, he felt an ache deeper than anything he had ever felt before.

"Emily, please," he whispered, his voice breaking. "Don't."

Tears slipped down her cheeks as she shook her head. "I'm sorry," she said softly, her heart shattering with every word. "I can't be her, Dennis. I can't be what you need me to be."

With that, she turned and walked away, leaving Dennis standing on the rooftop, staring after her with tears in his eyes. The noise of the party around him faded into nothing, and for the first time since Katarina had left, he felt the full weight of loss crash down on him.

Emily had been his lifeline, the person who had kept him afloat when he thought he might drown in his grief. And now, she was gone, and the emptiness that had been gnawing at him for so long finally swallowed him whole.

As he stood against the wall, he slowly sank to the ground, his feet like a locomotive in slow-motion bringing to his destination, hi hands trembling as he buried his face in them. He had lost her. He had lost them both. A weight no person should endure.

Someone I Used to Know

Years after Katarina and Dennis first started dating, Katarina had been hopeful, cautiously optimistic that they could build on what they originally had. She had thought that with enough time, patience, and understanding, they could find what they both desired.

But as the months went on, Katarina began to realize that no matter how much she wanted it to work, something was missing. She could feel it in the quiet moments they shared, moments that once felt natural but now seemed heavy with unspoken tension. They had both changed and no matter how much they tried to recreate what they once had, it just wasn't the same.

As the days with Dennis passed, Katarina found herself smiling more, but it was a smile she didn't quite recognize. There was a time when she had smiled effortlessly in his presence when the future felt certain and full of hope. But now, as much as she tried, there was a weight behind each smile, a heaviness she couldn't shake. In moments of quiet, when they were apart, she would sit by the window, tracing the condensation on the glass, wondering if love could evolve into something that no longer brought peace but confusion.

Katarina missed the simplicity of their early days, the way they could lose themselves in conversation for hours without a care in the world. But now, every word felt measured carefully. She wasn't the same person anymore—neither was he. And as much as she loved Dennis, she feared that love might no longer be enough."

Katarina sat on the edge of the bed one evening, staring at the picture frame on her nightstand. It was a photo of her and Dennis from years ago, back when they were still full of hope and possibility. The image was frozen in time, capturing a version of themselves that no longer existed. Katarina knew they had grown and evolved, but it was becoming clear that their paths had diverged in ways they hadn't fully anticipated.

She had been wrestling with her feelings for weeks now, trying to figure out where things had gone wrong. When she and Dennis had reconnected, there had been a spark—a flicker of the old magic that had once bound them so tightly. But over time, that spark had dimmed. They were both trying so hard to make it work, but it felt like they were holding onto something that had already slipped through their fingers.

Dennis, ever the optimist, had been determined to push forward. He was full of love, full of hope, always believing that they could get back to what they once had. But Katarina wasn't sure if she could match his enthusiasm anymore. She wasn't the same person she had been back then. And the more she tried to make herself fit into the life they were trying to rebuild, the more she realized how much she had changed.

It wasn't just about them as a couple—it was about her, too. The years she had spent away from Dennis had changed her in ways she hadn't fully understood until now. She had grown more independent, more focused on her career, and more certain of the things she wanted in life. And while she still loved Dennis, she couldn't shake the feeling that their relationship was holding her back from the version of herself she had worked so hard to become.

The real turning point came one evening after a particularly difficult day at work. Katarina had been dealing with a stressful project, and all she wanted was to come home, unwind, and have a quiet evening. But when she walked through the door, Dennis was there, his usual warmth and optimism on full display. He had made dinner, set the table, and was eager to hear about her day.

Katarina had smiled, grateful for his effort, but as they sat down to eat, she felt the tension building inside her. It wasn't Dennis's fault—he was being thoughtful caring, the way he always was—but the more they talked, the more Katarina realized how distant she felt from him. He was talking about their future, about the plans he had for them, but every word felt like a weight pressing down on her chest.

She could see the life he wanted for them—one where they stayed in Lake Caldwell, built a home, and maybe even started a family. But Katarina wasn't sure if that was the life she wanted anymore. She had tasted freedom and experienced life on her own terms, and now the idea of settling down in one place felt suffocating.

That night, as they lay in bed, Katarina couldn't sleep. She stared at the ceiling, her mind racing with thoughts of what her future might look like if she stayed with Dennis. She loved him—she had never stopped loving him—but love wasn't always enough. They had shared so much history so many memories, but those memories couldn't carry them through the future. They needed something more, and Katarina wasn't sure if they had it.

The next morning, Katarina knew she had to say something. The weight of her doubts had become too heavy to ignore, and she couldn't keep pretending that everything was fine.

"Dennis," she said softly as they sat at the breakfast table. "We need to talk."

Dennis looked up from his coffee, concern immediately clouding his face. "What's wrong?"

Katarina hesitated, trying to find the right words. "I've been thinking a lot lately… about us. About where we're headed."

Dennis's eyes softened, but there was a hint of worry behind them. "And?"

"And… I don't know if this is working," Katarina admitted, her voice trembling slightly. "We've been trying so hard, but it feels like we're holding onto something that's already gone."

Dennis set his coffee down, the worry in his expression deepening. "I thought we were doing okay. I mean, we've had some ups and downs, but that's normal, right?"

Katarina shook her head, tears welling up in her eyes. "It's not just that, Dennis. It's more than that. I love you, I do, but… I feel like we've changed. We're not the same people we were back then, and I don't know if we fit together the way we used to."

Dennis's face fell, and Katarina could see the hurt in his eyes. "So, what are you saying? That we're done?"

"I don't know," Katarina whispered, her voice breaking. "I just don't want to keep pretending that everything's okay when it's not. We need to be honest with ourselves and with each other."

Dennis sat back in his chair, his shoulders slumping as the weight of her words sank in. He rubbed his eye and felt tension in his neck, clearly struggling to process what she was saying.

"I don't want to lose you," he said quietly. "But I don't want to be with someone who's not sure if they want to be with me."

Katarina wiped away a tear, her heart aching at the pain she was causing him.

"I don't want to hurt you, Dennis. But I can't ignore these feelings anymore. I can't keep pretending that everything's fine when it's not."

For a long moment, they sat in silence, the distance between them feeling larger than ever.

Finally, Dennis spoke, his voice heavy with resignation. "I guess we need to figure out what's next then."

Katarina nodded, though her heart was breaking. She knew that this wasn't the end she had wanted, but it was the one that felt inevitable. They had both tried, but sometimes love wasn't enough to bridge the gap between who they were and who they had become.

As she stood up from the table, Katarina glanced back at Dennis, her heart aching with the knowledge that they were on the verge of losing each other again. But this time, it felt different. This time, it felt like the right choice, even if it hurt.

"I'm sorry," she whispered.

Dennis didn't say anything, but the sadness in his eyes spoke volumes.

Katarina left the house, feeling the weight of her decision settling on her shoulders. She knew that this was when they needed time apart to figure out who they were and what they really wanted. But as she walked away, a part of her wondered if she had just lost the one person who had ever truly understood her.

"All I Wanna Do"

The neon lights of the French Quarter in New Orleans blazed in the humid night, casting a colorful glow over the hordes of people that filled the narrow, historic street. Dennis found himself in the middle of it all, caught up in the intoxicating energy of New Orleans, a city that seemed to pulse with life even in the dead of night. The air was thick, the kind that clung to your skin and made everything feel more intense, more immediate.

"His phone buzzed with a notification. It was an email from a gallery in the city—an invitation to a new exhibit. He stared at it for a long moment, a strange pull of nostalgia washing over him. Art had been Katarina's world, one that he had always admired from a distance. He wondered if she would go. Perhaps she already had plans to be there, mingling with the crowd, her eyes glowing with the passion she always had for creativity."

"For a brief second, he considered going, too. But then, the weight of their last encounter at the bar pressed down on him. He shook his head and closed the email. No, New Orleans would be better. It was time to lose himself in a new city, surrounded by new faces, far away from the ghost of Katarina's smile."

Dennis had always been the responsible one, the friend who kept things under control, but tonight was different. He felt a wildness inside him, a need to let go of everything that had been holding him back. The alcohol flowed freely, dulling the edges of his pain, and the music thumped in his chest, syncing with the erratic beat of his heart.

Somewhere between the fifth and sixth bar, as the night blurred into a haze of lights and sound, Dennis saw her. She was standing at the edge of the crowd, her eyes locking with his for just a moment before she looked away. She was beautiful, with dark eyes and hair that framed her face and a confidence that radiated from her like heat.

Their eyes met again, and this time, neither looked away. There was an unspoken understanding between them, a mutual recognition of something they both needed at that moment. Dennis didn't hesitate— he walked over to her, the crowd parting like water as he moved, his mind racing. "It was a rainy night," he thought, even though the rain hadn't started yet.

"Hey," he said, his voice rough from shouting over the music all night.

"Hey," she replied, a slow smile spreading across her lips.

They didn't need to exchange many words. The connection between them was immediate, electric, and completely unburdened by expectations. There was no talk of past relationships, no discussions of what they did for a living, or where they were from. None of it mattered. All that mattered was the here and now, the heat between them, and the promise of what the night could bring.

"So, we found this hotel," he thought, the lyrics racing through his mind. "It was a place I knew well."

They left the bar together, the humid night air wrapping around them like a cloak as they stepped into the street. The sky above was heavy with clouds, and the faint rumble of thunder in the distance hinted at a coming storm. But neither of them cared. They walked together, side by side until they found a quiet alleyway away from the noise and the crowds.

The rain started to fall, slowly at first, warm drops that sizzled on their heated skin. Dennis pulled her close, their bodies pressing together as the rain began to pour in earnest. The storm that had been brewing all night finally broke, and with it, so did their restraint.

They kissed with a fierce, desperate passion, "I am the flower; you are the seed," she whispered in his ear, the words a perfect reflection of the moment, the rain mingling with their sweat as they gave in to the moment. There was no tenderness here, no promises of love or a future together. This was pure, unfiltered desire—two people finding solace in each other's arms, if only for one night.

Dennis could feel the fire in her touch, the same fire that burned in him. They moved together, their breath coming in ragged gasps as they lost themselves in the heat of the moment, "All I wanna do is make love to you," she whispered once more. The rain continued to fall, soaking them to the bone, but it only seemed to add to the intensity of their connection.

For that brief time, nothing else existed. There was no past, no future—just the here and now, the sensation of her body against his, the taste of rain on her lips, and the rhythm of their hearts beating in time with the storm.

And then, as suddenly as it had begun, it was over. They stood there for a moment, catching their breath, the reality of what had just happened slowly sinking in. Dennis looked at her, and she looked back at him, both knowing that this was it. There would be no exchange of numbers, no promises to meet again.

She smiled at him, a soft, almost wistful smile, and Dennis felt a pang of something deep inside—a mix of regret and relief. This wasn't love; it wasn't meant to be anything more than what it was.

"Goodbye," she whispered, her voice barely audible over the sound of the rain.

"Goodbye," he replied, watching as she turned and walked away, disappearing into the night.

Dennis stood there for a moment longer, letting the rain wash over him before he finally turned and made his way back to his friends.

The night had given him what he needed—a release, a moment of escape. But as he walked back into the thrumming energy of Bourbon Street, he couldn't help but feel a little emptier than before, as if the fire that had burned so brightly just moments ago had left behind nothing but ash.

But he didn't dwell on it. This night, this moment would be just another memory, another story to tuck away and move on from. There would be no tomorrow for them, and that was exactly how it was meant to be.

The Peaks and Valleys of Emotions

Katarina's life since leaving Dennis had been a whirlwind of moments—some thrilling, some disappointing, but none of them truly fulfilling. The months had stretched into a year of blind dates, spontaneous adventures, and nights spent in the company of strangers who tried but failed to fill the empty space Dennis had once occupied. She had thrown herself into the dating world with reckless abandon, convinced that if she pushed hard enough, she could forget him.

Her first few dates were exhilarating. There was the lawyer from Boston, charming but too self-absorbed to notice her quiet moments of hesitation. Then, the photographer she met at a gallery, who had seemed perfect—artistic, passionate, and eager to explore her every whim. But even with the spark of newness, the excitement never lasted. She found herself walking home from dinners and drinks, feeling more alone than she had when she'd left Dennis.

The nights were the worst. Katarina wasn't a stranger to the kind of loneliness that creeps in when the world quiets down, but this was different. Every time she slipped between the sheets, the coldness of her empty bed reminded her that she was still searching for something—or rather, someone—she couldn't quite let go of. She tried to fill that void with fleeting moments of physical connection, thinking that maybe if she could just lose herself in someone else's arms, the memory of Dennis would finally fade.

But it never did.

There was one night when she had gone out with a group of friends to a trendy new bar in the city. The music pulsed through her body as she danced with a man she'd met earlier that evening. He was handsome— tall and confident in a way that made her forget, for a moment, the void in her heart. His hands lingered on her waist, pulling her closer as they moved together on the dance floor. The chemistry was undeniable, and yet, with every beat of the music, she found herself drifting back to the thoughts of Dennis.

They had danced like this once in a dimly lit bar on a summer night. She remembered how safe she had felt in his arms, how everything had seemed to melt away when they were together. But that feeling was gone now, and as she let the stranger's lips brush against her neck, all she felt was a hollow ache where warmth should have been.

After a few more drinks, they stumbled back to his apartment. It was small, messy, and smelled faintly of cologne and stale takeout. Katarina followed him to the bedroom, telling herself this was what she needed—just a warm body, someone to make her forget the past, if only for a few hours. But as they lay together afterward, his arm draped lazily over her, she stared up at the ceiling, wide awake and filled with regret. His touch had been mechanical, devoid of the tenderness she craved, and once again, her mind wandered back to Dennis.

She slipped out of the bed quietly, gathering her clothes and slipping into them in the dark. As she tiptoed out of the apartment and into the cool night air, a "walk of shame," you could say. She felt a familiar pang of sadness. She had hoped that by now, she would have moved on, that she would have found someone who could ignite the same fire in her that Dennis once had. But it hadn't happened. No one came close.

It wasn't that she hadn't tried. She had gone on countless dates, each one beginning with the hope that this time would be different, that this man would be the one to make her forget. But every single date ended the same way—with a sense of emptiness that only grew with each passing day.

Her friends had started to notice the pattern. Over brunch, one Sunday, her best friend, Karen, leaned in and asked the question Katarina had been dreading. "Kat, what's going on with you? You've been on so many dates, but you always seem…disconnected. Is it just about finding someone new, or is there something else?"

Katarina sighed, pushing her food around on her plate. "I don't know, Karen. I thought this would be easier. I thought I'd feel something for someone by now. But every time I'm with someone else, it's like…I'm just going through the motions."

"You're still thinking about him, aren't you? Dennis?" said Katrina.

The mention of his name made Katarina's chest tighten. She nodded slowly. "Yeah. I guess I am. It's stupid, right? I was the one who left. I was the one who said I needed space. But no matter how many people I meet, I keep coming back to him."

Karen reached across the table, placing a comforting hand on Katarina's. "It's not stupid. You can't just switch off feelings like that. But, Kat, you have to figure out what you really want. Are you trying to move on, or are you just avoiding the fact that maybe you're still in love with him?"

The words hit her like a punch to the gut. Was that what she had been doing? Avoiding the truth? She had told herself that leaving Dennis was the right decision and that she needed time to figure out who she was without him. But now, she wasn't so sure. As she sat there, staring at her reflection in her coffee cup, she realized something terrifying: no matter how many men she dated, no matter how many nights she spent searching for a connection, her heart always found its way back to Dennis.

She thought about the way he used to hold her, the way his eyes would light up when he looked at her as if she was the only person in the world. She missed that. She missed him. But she had left him. She had walked away, thinking that space was what she needed, that she would find herself in the arms of someone else. Now, after all this time, she realized that maybe she hadn't been searching for someone new—maybe she had been searching for a way back to him.

The blind dates, the casual hookups, the fleeting attempts at fulfilling sexual fantasies—they had all been distractions. But none of them had made her feel what she had felt with Dennis. She had been chasing an idea, a fantasy of what she thought she wanted, but now, in the quiet moments when she was alone with her thoughts, she couldn't deny the truth.

Katarina stood up from the table, her heart heavy but clearer than it had been in a long time. She needed to stop running from the past. She needed to face the fact that no one else had ever made her feel the way Dennis had, and maybe, just maybe, that was something worth fighting for.

As she walked home that evening, the city lights twinkling in the distance, Katarina decided. She wasn't sure if it was too late or if Dennis would even want to see her again, but maybe she should try if that moment were to present itself.

Highway to the Sun

Hungary had never been at the top of Dennis's travel list, but something about visiting there in the summer felt right after the past 100 years it felt like he'd had. He wanted to get away, to escape the weight of everything that had settled so heavily on his shoulders.

The warmth of the season, the unfamiliar streets, and the chance to leave behind the familiar faces and memories—all of it seemed like exactly what he needed. He craved something real, something that would bring him back to life.

The mornings were always the hardest for Dennis. He would wake up, staring at the floor while lying on his stomach, feeling that empty space beside him in bed.

"Recently, it's the morning when I feel her absence the most."

He thought, the ache of Katarina's absence still lingering in his chest. He missed her laughter—how it used to fill the room, how it used to fill him.

"I long for her laughter, so long after it's faded away."

There was no comfort in the tears he cried, no peace in the sadness that clung to him.

He wished he could find just one person to explain why things had turned out the way they had. Why it felt like every time he thought he had moved on, the memories would sneak up on him again.

Hungary, though, felt like a good place to lose himself for a while. The vast open skies, the rolling hills, and the quiet villages seemed to offer the freedom he sought.

"I just want to wake up under the wide, open sky."

Dennis thought, longing to feel something real again before it was too late. There was a part of him that needed to believe that he wasn't doomed to carry the weight of his past forever.

He spent his days wandering through Budapest, the streets lined with history and life.

The sun shone brightly, its warmth a welcome contrast to the cold ache that had settled in his chest. He would sit by the Danube River, watching the boats drift by, and feel the pull of time.

The city was alive with tourists, locals, and children running about, but Dennis felt a quiet detachment from it all.

"These days, it's in the evenings that I really feel the weight of time," he realized.

In the quiet of twilight, when the light began to fade and the night crept in, he felt the weight of everything—his sorrows, his joys, his fears. The days seemed to stretch on endlessly, and the memories of Katarina and all the moments of his life played over in his mind like a song on repeat.

He would hear children singing songs and playing games in the streets. They laughed without care, completely unaware of the grown-up who was learning the painful lessons of life just a few feet away.

"They don't understand that the grown-up is learning how to hurt."

He thought with a sigh. He was still learning how to move forward, how to heal, and how to make sense of the years that had brought him so much love and so much loss.

One evening, Dennis decided to take a drive through the countryside. The roads stretched out before him, winding through fields of sunflowers and small villages, the sky above glowing with the colors of the setting sun.

"I just want to wake up beneath that vast, open sky."

He thought as the breeze rushed through the open windows of his rental car. For the first time in months, he felt a flicker of hope stir inside him. He didn't know where he was going, but that was okay. He had miles and miles yet to run, and for once, he didn't feel the need to have all the answers.

"I don't know where I'm going, but I've got miles and miles yet to run."

As the sun dipped lower in the sky, casting long shadows over the landscape, Dennis found himself driving along a quiet, winding road that seemed to lead nowhere. But he didn't care.

 The freedom of the moment, the simple joy of being alive and on the road, was enough.

"I just want to experience something real before my times runs out."

He whispered to himself as he watched the horizon stretch out endlessly before him.

Hungary had given him something he hadn't expected—a sense of peace, however fleeting. He felt lighter as he drove as if he had left a piece of his past behind in the city streets.

The pain of the past wasn't gone, but it felt less heavy. And as the car moved along the empty highway, Dennis felt the pull of possibility.

"Won't you come with me on the road that leads to the sun?"

He thought, smiling to himself. There was something out there for him, something waiting beyond the miles of road and endless skies. He didn't know what it was yet, but for the first time in a long time, he was ready to find out.

"Sometime Around Midnight"

It was just after midnight when Dennis found himself at the bar, the soft glow of the lights above casting a warm haze over the crowd. The night had stretched on longer than he had expected. He had met up with a few friends for a drink, hoping to unwind after another long day. The noise of the band, the clinking of glasses, and the distractions of numerous conversations all blurred together, lulling him into a comfortable numbness. But as the minutes ticked by, he began to lose himself, if only for a minute or two.

The bar was crowded, packed with people all looking for a way to forget themselves for a while. As the band played a slow, melancholy tune, Dennis leaned against the bar, nursing his drink. The piano's notes struck a chord deep inside him, the sound a reflection of the ache he tried to keep buried. It was a song about forgetting, and tonight, that's exactly what he wanted to do.

But then, out of the corner of his eye, he saw her. The air seemed to crackle. A shiver ran down his spine, and his breath hitched. Katarina, her white dress a beacon in the dim light, stood near the far end of the bar, her laughter a melody that seemed to echo through the crowded space. He watched, his heart pounding, as she moved, her head tilted back, a strand of hair falling over her shoulder, catching the light. The sight of her was a blow, a sudden burst of color that shattered the carefully constructed walls he'd built around his heart. He wanted to look away, to turn back to the comforting anonymity of the crowd, but he couldn't. He was frozen, trapped in the moment, unable to pull himself out of the flood of memories.

He hadn't seen her for what felt like an eternity. He wasn't expecting her to be here, in this bar, on this night. But there she was, standing under the bar lights, wearing that white dress he remembered so well. And in that instant, everything changed.

For a moment, the room spun, and Dennis found it hard to catch his breath. It was like the air had been sucked out of the room, leaving him dizzy and off-balance. He watched as she laughed, her head thrown back, her smile as radiant as ever. She was holding her drink— a tonic, just like she always did—cradling it in her hands like it was some kind of lifeline. And even though she hadn't seen him yet, he knew she was watching. She always had a way of knowing when he was near, even before she could see him.

The music swelled, the band continuing to play that song, but all Dennis could hear was the pounding of his own heart. His emotions swirled inside him, rushing to the surface like waves crashing onto the shore. Every memory, every touch, every whispered word they had ever shared came flooding back with a force that nearly knocked him over.

And then, just like that, Katarina turned. Their eyes met across the room, and in that moment, time seemed to slow. She smiled softly, and the sight of it sent a shiver down Dennis's spine. He felt lost, hopeless, caught in the haze of the wine he had been sipping all night. The memories of their past came rushing back—memories of the nights they spent entwined in each other's arms, bodies curling together like two perfect circles.

As Katarina began to walk toward him, the room seemed to spin again. She moved with that same graceful ease, every step measured and confident. Dennis could feel the shift in the air, the change in his emotions overwhelming him. He wanted to turn away, to avoid whatever was coming next, but he couldn't. He was frozen, trapped in the moment, unable to pull himself out of the flood of memories.

And then she was there, standing right in front of him.

"Dennis," she said softly, her voice just loud enough to be heard over the music.

He swallowed hard, trying to keep his composure. "Katarina," he replied, his voice rougher than he intended.

She smiled again, that same smile that had once melted every wall he had built around his heart. He could smell her perfume, a scent that was so familiar it hurt. The last time he had been this close to her, she had been lying in his arms, their bodies pressed together in the quiet of the night. And now, here she was, standing inches away from him, bringing with her the weight of every emotion he had tried to bury.

"How are you?" she asked, her eyes searching his face for something—maybe recognition, maybe regret.

"I'm…" He trailed off, unsure of how to answer. "I'm standing in front of you," he said with a slight chuckle. But deep down, he was speechless.

Before he could say anything more, Katarina took a small step closer. The room seemed to close in around them, the sounds of the bar fading into the background. Dennis could feel the heat of her body, could see the way her eyes sparkled in the dim light. And just like that, every memory they had shared rushed back—like feral waves crashing into his mind.

He could see her lying next to him, her body curled against him, their legs tangled together under the sheets. He could feel the way their hearts had once beat in time, the way her breath had felt against his skin. And now, standing here, he was reminded of all the ways he had lost her, of all the ways he had tried to forget.

But forgetting had never been an option. Not really.

Katarina looked at him for a long moment, and then, with a softness that made Dennis's chest ache, she reached out and touched his arm. "I've missed you," she whispered.

Her words were like a knife to his heart, reopening wounds that had never fully healed. "I've missed you as well," he said in a confused, hesitant manner. "Sometimes I would find the phone in my hand staring at your number, you know?"

The room continued to spin, the wine clouding his thoughts and the music a distant echo in the back of his mind. But all Dennis could focus on was Katarina—her touch, her scent, her presence—and the overwhelming sense of loss that threatened to swallow him whole.

Katarina kept staring while gently touching his shoulder, "I better get back," she said. "Yeah, I mean, of course," Dennis said with a blank stare and a look of wonder in his eyes. As she walked away, they both knew it was not for the last time, again.

Bleeding Love

It had been weeks since Dennis saw Katarina at the bar, but the encounter had left its mark. Some days, he hardly thought about it at all, going about his life as if nothing had changed. But on other days, the memory hit him with the force of a tidal wave, pulling him under and reminding him of all the emotions he had worked so hard to bury.

He had been afraid of this day for so long, the day when his carefully constructed world would start to unravel. After Katarina, he had closed himself off from love, convinced that the pain wasn't worth the risk. Once or twice had been enough to teach him that love could be a brutal, cutting thing. He had told himself he didn't need it, didn't want it anymore. Time passed, and before he knew it, he had built walls so high around his heart that he had almost forgotten what it felt like to let someone in.

But that morning at the bar, when he saw Katarina standing there, everything changed. It was as if time stopped, and for the first time in what felt like forever, his heart melted. The walls he had built so carefully began to crumble, and all the memories—the love, the heartbreak, the joy—came flooding back in. He tried to play it cool, tried to pretend like seeing her didn't matter, but it did. It mattered more than he was willing to admit.

At first, he convinced himself it was nothing, just a fluke, a random coincidence that didn't mean anything. But as the days passed, he found himself thinking about her more and more. Her face haunted his thoughts, the way she looked at him, the memories of their time together that never truly faded.

He had worked so hard to forget, to put his life back together after everything fell apart. But seeing Katarina again had opened old wounds, and now he was bleeding love all over again. The pain was familiar, but it felt different this time. It wasn't sharp and piercing like it had been when they first broke up. It was a slow, dull ache, a reminder of everything they had once shared.

Dennis couldn't shake the feeling that seeing Katarina again was more than just a chance encounter. He tried to brush it off, telling himself that it didn't mean anything. But deep down, he knew the truth—he wasn't over her. He had never been over her. No matter how much time had passed, no matter how hard he had tried to move on, she still had a hold on him.

Some nights, as he lay awake, he could hear the voices in his head— his friends, his family—telling him that he was crazy, that he needed to let her go. They didn't understand. They never had. To them, Katarina was just a part of his past, a chapter he had closed long ago. But for Dennis, she was so much more than that. She was the one who had cut him open, who had left him bleeding, and no matter how hard he tried to heal, the scars were always there, just beneath the surface.

He could hear the doubts creeping in, the way people had always tried to pull him away from her, telling him that he deserved better, that he should move on. But they didn't know the truth. They didn't know what it was like to love someone so deeply, so completely, that it hurt. They didn't know what it was like to carry the weight of that love, even when it felt like it was tearing you apart.

In the quiet moments, when the noise of the world faded away, all he could see was her face. The way she had smiled at him when things were good, the way her laugh had filled the room, the way they had once fit together so perfectly. And even though they were no longer together, even though they had gone their separate ways, he still felt that connection, that invisible thread that tied him to her.

He tried to ignore it, tried to distract himself with work, with friends, with anything that would keep his mind off her. But no matter what he did, she was always there, lingering in the back of his mind, in the corners of his heart.

And every time he thought he had finally gotten over her, every time he thought he was ready to move on, the wound would open again, and he would find himself bleeding love all over again.

Dennis didn't know what to do. He had spent so long trying to convince himself that he was better off without her, that he didn't need her in his life anymore. But the truth was, no matter how hard he tried to close the door on their past, Katarina was always there, just beyond the threshold, waiting for him.

And now, after seeing her again, after feeling the old emotions stir within him, he wasn't sure if he could keep pretending that he didn't care. Maybe he had never stopped caring. Maybe, just maybe, he had been bleeding love this entire time, and he had only just realized it.

As the weeks went by, Dennis found himself torn between two worlds—the life he had built for himself without her and the memories of the love they had shared. He knew that seeing Katarina again had reopened wounds he had thought were healed, and now, he had to decide whether he was going to keep bleeding or if it was time to finally let go.

But letting go wasn't easy. It never had been. Because when it came to Katarina, no matter how hard he tried, she would always be the one who cut him open. And he would keep bleeding love for as long as it took to heal.

I Can't Fight This Feeling

It had been weeks since Dennis saw Katarina at that bar, but his mind hadn't stopped racing since. Every day, he replayed the moment they had locked eyes across the room, the way she had smiled, that small, uncertain smile, and the flood of emotions that had surged through him. He had tried to forget it, to push it aside like all the other memories of her, but this time was different. The encounter had shaken something loose inside him, something he could no longer ignore.

He had been fighting this feeling for years—convincing himself that he had moved on, that what they had was part of the past. But seeing her again had undone all the progress he thought he had made. "I can't fight this feeling any longer," he thought to himself, sitting at his kitchen table, staring at his phone. He had been rehearsing the words he wanted to say, imagining what it would be like to call her, to see her again.

The bar had been packed that night, the dim lights and chatter offering a sense of anonymity that made Dennis feel like he could breathe. He hadn't expected to see her there. In fact, he had been out with friends, trying to forget the weight of the last few months. But then, there she was, standing near the far end of the bar, holding a glass of wine, laughing with a group of people. The sight of her had caught him off guard, and for a moment, he felt like the air had been knocked out of him.

"And I feel like I can't let go," he thought, remembering how he had stood frozen, watching her. He had told himself that he wouldn't get caught up in it again, that seeing her was just a coincidence. But the longer he stood there, the more he realized that his heart wasn't going to let him off the hook so easily.

He had tried to go about his night, talking with his friends, pretending not to notice her just a few feet away. But the truth was, he couldn't focus on anything else. His mind kept wandering back to her—the sound of her laughter cutting through the noise, the way she tucked her hair behind her ear, the memories of the nights they had spent together when everything had felt so right. "What started out as friendship has grown stronger," he thought, and he knew he couldn't keep pretending it was just the past.

As the night went on, he had tried to avoid her, but the inevitable happened. Their eyes met across the bar, and just like that, the walls he had built around his heart began to crumble. "I only wish I had the strength to let it show," he mused, his thoughts racing.

She had walked over to him, tentative at first like she wasn't sure if she should. But when she was just a few feet away, she smiled that same familiar smile that had always made his heart skip a beat. "Dennis," she had said softly, her voice barely cutting through the din of the bar.

Hearing her say his name had unlocked something in him that he had been holding back for too long. He had smiled, though it had felt shaky, and replied, "Katarina."

They had exchanged small talk, the kind of conversation that felt forced, full of things that didn't really matter. All the while, Dennis's mind had been racing. He could smell her perfume, the same scent he remembered from the nights they had spent together. He could hear her laughter, see the way she looked at him, and feel the weight of all the unsaid things between them.

"I can't fight this feeling any longer," he thought as she asked him how he was doing, how life had been. His emotions swirled inside him, and all the memories came rushing back like waves crashing against the shore. He had tried to run from this for so long, but seeing her here now made it impossible to deny.

He had stood there, trying to keep his composure, but inside, he was unraveling. "I've forgotten what I started fighting for," he realized. It wasn't about letting go or moving on. He had been fighting against himself, against his own feelings, and now he wasn't sure why he had ever tried.

The conversation had been brief, just long enough for him to feel the pull of their past but not long enough to resolve anything. She had smiled at him again before walking away, her presence lingering like a ghost, leaving him feeling both hollow and full of hope at the same time.

Now, sitting alone at his kitchen table, the glow of the city lights flickering through the window, Dennis couldn't stop thinking about her. "Even as I wander, I'm keeping you in sight," he thought, realizing that no matter how far he had gone, no matter how much time had passed, Katarina had always been there, just beneath the surface, waiting for him to stop running.

"I can't fight this feeling anymore." The truth was inescapable. He couldn't push her away, couldn't pretend that seeing her again hadn't stirred up every emotion he had tried to suppress. The love he felt for her, the longing for what they had—it was all still there, just as strong as ever. And now, he knew he had to do something about it.

He picked up his phone, his heart pounding in his chest. He had rehearsed this moment a hundred times, but now that it was here, all the words he had prepared seemed to vanish. He stared at her number, the screen glowing in the dim light of his apartment.

"I can't fight this feeling anymore." It echoed in his mind as he pressed the call button, his heart racing as the phone rang once, twice, and then...

"Hello?"

Katarina's voice on the other end sent a rush of emotions through him. He took a deep breath, his heart pounding in his chest. "Katarina," he said softly. "It's Dennis."

There was a pause, and he could almost hear her processing the moment. "Dennis..." she said, her voice filled with surprise. "I didn't expect to hear from you."

"I know," he replied, the words coming slowly. "I didn't plan on calling, but... I've been thinking about you. About us."

Another pause. The silence on the other end was deafening, but then she spoke, her voice barely a whisper. "I've been thinking about you too."

And just like that, the weight of the past weeks, months, and years began to lift. "And if I have to crawl upon the floor, come crashing through your door," Dennis thought, his heart swelling with hope. This time, he wasn't going to run. He wasn't going to fight it.

He couldn't fight this feeling anymore.

Open Arms

Five weeks had passed since that fateful first phone call, and Dennis's world had shifted in ways he couldn't have predicted. It started with late-night conversations, each one testing the fragile waters between him and Katarina. They would talk for hours, laughing about old memories, trading stories of the lives they had lived apart, their words an unspoken bridge reconnecting the gap that time had created. At first, it was cautious—two people standing on the edges of something familiar yet changed. But as the days slipped into nights, the distance between them seemed to fade.

Yet, for all the ease in their conversations, there was something unspoken beneath the surface. In the pauses, in the moments when their words hung heavy in the air, Dennis felt it—a lingering doubt, a fear that perhaps too much time had passed. He would catch Katarina looking at him, her eyes searching for something, a question unasked, her lips parting as if to speak, only to close again. And in those moments, Dennis wondered if time had truly healed the wounds or if they had only been buried, waiting to resurface.

One evening, after watching the season finale of The Great British Bake Off on her couch, Dennis finally asked the question that had been gnawing at him for weeks. "Are we really doing this, Katarina? Or are we just pretending everything is okay?"

His words cut through the quiet, hanging in the air between them like a fragile thread. Katarina's eyes drifted to the window as if searching for the answer in the glow of the city lights. The silence stretched on until she finally spoke, her voice soft but unsure. "I don't know… but I want to try."

It wasn't the certainty Dennis had hoped for, but it was honest. It was raw. And for now, it was enough.

They began seeing each other more often, dipping their toes back into the life they had once shared. Dinners at small restaurants and late-night walks along the waterfront were all filled with the kind of conversation that felt both familiar and new. There was a tenderness between them now, one that hadn't been there before, as if they both understood the fragility of what they were rebuilding. The love they had shared hadn't disappeared; it had simply been buried under the weight of time and distance. But now, like an old photograph found in an attic, it was being dusted off and brought back into the light.

Still, neither of them could ignore the changes. They weren't the same people they had been before. Both had grown had lived through their own private storms, and it was impossible to pretend otherwise. But it was in those changes that they found something new, something deeper. The passion that had once burned brightly between them was now tempered with a maturity they hadn't had before—a quiet understanding that love wasn't just about the highs but about navigating the lows together.

One night, after a quiet dinner at a small bistro by the water, Dennis found himself back at Katarina's apartment, sitting beside her on the couch. The city stretched out before them through the window, the lights twinkling like a thousand tiny stars, and in the stillness of the night, Dennis felt a sense of peace he hadn't known in years. Katarina leaned into him, resting her head on his shoulder, her hand intertwined with his. Her breath was soft against his skin, and for the first time in a long time, Dennis felt like he was exactly where he was meant to be.

"How did we let things get so far apart?" Katarina's voice was barely a whisper, filled with the weight of years of missed chances and unspoken words. "I never stopped thinking about you."

Dennis turned his head slightly, his lips brushing against her hair. He inhaled the familiar scent of her, a mixture of vanilla and something uniquely her own. "Neither did I," he murmured, his voice thick with emotion. "I never stopped loving you. I just didn't know how to say it."

The words hung between them, heavy with the truth they had both been avoiding. So much time had passed, so many nights spent apart, both of them trying to move on, to convince themselves that the other was just a memory. But here, at this moment, all of that seemed irrelevant. What mattered was the connection they still felt, the love that had never really faded.

"I missed you," Dennis whispered, his hand tightening around hers. "I thought I could forget, but I couldn't. Every day, I'd think about calling you, but I was too afraid."

Katarina lifted her head to meet his gaze, her eyes glistening with unshed tears. "I was afraid, too. Afraid that it was too late, that we'd lost something we couldn't get back."

Dennis reached up, gently cupping her cheek, his thumb brushing away a single tear that had slipped free. "We haven't lost anything," he said softly. "We're still here. We still have this."

For a moment, they simply stared at each other, their faces inches apart, the weight of their pasts between them. And then, slowly, Katarina leaned forward, her lips finding him in a kiss that was both familiar and new. It wasn't the desperate, passionate kiss of their younger days but something deeper, something that spoke of love, forgiveness, and the promise of a future together.

When they finally pulled away, Katarina smiled, her eyes bright with emotion. "I've been waiting for you to say that," she whispered, her voice filled with a quiet joy that Dennis hadn't heard in years.

The tension between them melted away, replaced by a sense of peace, of finally finding their way back to each other after so many years apart. They had made mistakes and taken different paths, but now they were here, together again, and this time, there was nothing standing in their way.

Dennis wrapped his arms around her, pulling her close, feeling the steady rhythm of her heartbeat against his chest. The weight of the past—the years of separation, the nights spent wondering what could have been—dissolved in that moment. He wasn't afraid anymore. He knew what he wanted. He wanted her. He had always wanted her.

"I'm done hiding how I feel," he said, his voice full of conviction. "I'm done running. I want us to be together, Katarina. No more doubts, no more second-guessing. I'm coming to you with open arms."

Katarina rested her forehead against his, her breath warm against his lips. "I'm not going anywhere, Dennis," she whispered. "We're in this together."

They sat like that for what felt like hours, wrapped in each other's arms, the world outside forgotten. The future stretched out before them, full of possibilities. They didn't need to rush. They didn't need to force anything. They had time—time to rebuild what they had lost, time to create something new, something stronger.

As the night deepened, Katarina shifted in his arms, her voice soft but steady. "Do you remember the night we danced in the rain?" she asked, a smile tugging at the corners of her lips.

Dennis chuckled, the memory of that wild, impromptu night flooding back. They had been caught in a summer storm, soaked to the skin, but neither of them had cared. They had danced in the downpour, laughing like children, spinning each other around as if the world had stopped just for them. "How could I forget?" he said, smiling. "It's one of my favorite memories."

Katarina's smile widened. "Mine too. I think that's when I realized I was in love with you. When I knew that I wanted to spend the rest of my life with you."

Dennis felt his heart swell at her words. "And here we are," he said, pulling her even closer. "Ready to write the next chapter of our story."

The weight of their past was gone, replaced by the certainty of their future. As they sat together, wrapped in the warmth of each other's embrace, Dennis knew one thing for certain—this time, he wasn't letting go. They had found their way back to each other, and no matter what challenges lay ahead, they would face them together.

With open arms.

Epilogue

Years later, their lives intertwined in a way they never could have imagined. The memories of their past, the laughter, the pain, the heartache, and the love were still woven into the fabric of who they were.

Dennis and Katarina had learned that love is not always easy. It doesn't always unfold as planned, and sometimes, the paths to healing are long and winding.

But, they learned, too, that love can endure. It can survive even the most devastating losses and the deepest hurts, and it can always, always find a way to bring two souls back together.

They knew that no matter what life threw their way, they would face it together, with open arms, their hearts forever bound by a love that had survived against all odds.

www.ingramcontent.com/pod-product-compliance
Lightning Source LLC
Chambersburg PA
CBHW040202160726
48006CB00014B/1859